POCKET POS

Big Ideas For Delivering
Positively Outrageous Service

T. Scott Gross

MASTERMEDIA LIMITED
NEW YORK

Designed by Michael Woyton
Manufactured in the United States of America
10 9 8 7 6 5 4 3 2 1

Positively Outrageous Service defined:

☆ Random and unexpected
☆ Out of proportion to the circumstance
☆ Invites the customer to play or be otherwise highly involved
☆ Creates compelling, positive word-of-mouth

POS

The inner secret of POS: It establishes a personal relationship between the server and the served.

Unexpected is the key to POS. It's the element of surprise and novelty that grabs the attention of the customer and creates an experience that's memorable because it's so different from the expectation.

Random rewards create regular behavior.

What could you do to surprise your customers?

POS is a marketing strategy.

Traditional marketing begets trial. But POS begets repeat business. Ultimately your marketing strategies live or die within your own four walls.

POS

Any ideas for making your service strategy a marketing strategy?

The big fish do eat little fish. That's the way it has always been. The problem isn't what *size* you are. It's what *kind* of fish you are that counts.

Little fish don't get eaten simply because they are little. It's more a matter of being in the wrong place at the wrong time.

If you're a little fish, don't even dream of beating 'em on price.

Service, Positively Outrageous Service is the advantage that belongs to the littlest, most responsive fish. Little fish that serve outrageously swim rings around the competition.

POS

What can you do that the bigger fish cannot? This could be your competitive advantage!

A creative entrepreneurial spirit occupying a position of corporate power can set even large organizations buzzing.

Who are the entrepreneurs in your organization?

What could happen if you turned them loose?

In an age when the aspects of quality that can be measured by the physical sciences will be ever more standardized, the social interaction of service will acquire increasing significance.

A product that works according to design is not necessarily a product that is designed according to the work. Only those companies with the closest relationship with the customer will be able to design products that most accurately target customer needs.

POS

How would your customers modify your product or service?

It's important to notice that even budget-conscious, do-it-yourself types are no longer settling for sub-par products.

They expect quality.

Quality service is quality product.

Dollars saved at the discounters are waiting to fall into the hands of businesses offering personal-touch, boutique-style services.

When things can be custom-produced at will, there will be a rising demand for custom service as well.

POS

How could you customize your service?

Any business that doesn't have a system for customer feedback is a solution looking for a problem.

Always try to say yes to a customer. Say no when it's for their own good.

Complaints are requests to get it right, to keep your promise.

Are you asking for complaints?

Every sale carries with it a promise. With service the promise is often only implied.

Funny thing about service: It's a major portion of product cost, but rarely mentioned on the packaging.

POS

What aspects of service could you mention on your packaging? *(Think! Think!)*

Treated properly, a supplier can be a major asset.

We are all customers.

An open market is a democratic market where customers vote at the cash register.

Excellent or perhaps just good service delivered by the owner, president or grand Pooh Bah takes on outrageous proportions simply because such people add their personal status to the event.

It's possible to double your sales without adding a single new customer. All that must be done is to make your current customers feel so good about doing business with you that they come in twice as often.

Is the boss in the office — or on the floor?

Serving outrageously almost always involves an element of risk.

Listen to your customers. Give them exactly what they want, any way they want it. And invite them to participate in their own service.

Positively Outrageous Service is highly memorable and that, my friends, is positioning.

POS

What could be done to make your service "memorable"?

When confronted with the need to fill a vacancy, executives look at the pool of available talent. Instead of finding a superior candidate, they often hire the candidate who is merely the least offensive.

You want your competition to be at least pretty good. Otherwise you could end up being painted with the same broad brush as the others.

Serving fun is a great way to earn top-of-mind positioning.

That's not to say that you shouldn't be absolutely fanatical about product and service quality.

Just remember to have fun while you are at it!

---POS---

How could your service be fun?
How could working for you be fun?

Anyone can give away product.

It takes brains to sell it! (Anonymous)

Discounting is a short-term cover-up of long-term problems. If you must discount to survive, your prices are too high, your service is too poor or your quality is too low.

Discount and it won't be long before the customer figures out what your product is really worth.

If a vendor isn't knocking on your door to offer assistance, then you should either knock on his door or look for a vendor who is truly interested in your success.

Perhaps the best sources of ideas will be found outside your industry. Granted, it's not likely that you will find ideas that you can steal intact. But you will find ideas.

What idea/services could your vendors supply?

Doing what is right and good for the customer is the best thing to do. If you do it because you love others, that's fine. You'll receive the recognition you deserve.

If you do good things solely for the recognition, that's also fine. At least you did something good that made a difference.

In reality there are only so many potential new customers in your market. Discounting is the lazy approach to promotion.

Four guidelines for promotions:
1. Have fun.
2. Get people to your store.
3. Get people involved with your product.
4. Do something good for others.

POS

Hint: Take two ordinary promotion ideas and mix them together!

Fun or not, promotions should never be allowed to interfere with quality product and service.

We do not participate in any promotional effort that does not have as its ultimate goal to get people into our store. Period.

Promotions that put your product in your customers' hands will result in sales.

A taste test is the ultimate promotion.

How can you get customers to "taste" your product?

Your product is your business, and at the very least, a donation should expose more people to your product. Give product for a group to use or auction.

If you must make a donation: Donate product.

How could you creatively donate product?

Look around. You may be surprised at how many partners you have with a major interest in your success.

The best promotions are those in which everyone is a winner.

Everyone likes to have a good time, but not everyone wants to participate personally.

Sometimes the only way you can measure the effectiveness of a marketing strategy is to stop.

Remember your customers even when they are not buying.

Support causes the customer holds important.

Say you're sorry for the slightest slip from standard. Ask for the customer's opinion.

List six ways to say you are sorry.
(Go ahead—Do it!)

When you are too busy to love on the customers, you are too darned busy. Your unloved customers will help you get things back in balance by staying away, so that you'll have fewer customers to worry over.

Be a product and service quality fanatic. Nothing tells the customer that she is important like being fanatical over getting the product, service, and order perfect.

People don't like to wait. Make waiting an experience and delays won't be noticed!

POS

What could you do to turn a wait into an experience?

The best thing to do is to eliminate waits. The next best thing is to make them disappear by entertaining the customer.

If you really want to offend someone, treat him as though his time — and therefore he — is of no value or consequence.

Demonstrate that the customer is first by respecting his time.

POS

What "waits" could you totally eliminate?

If you really want to WOW the customer, treat his time as a precious commodity.

What is worse than waiting in a long line? Waiting in a long line when all you need is a question answered or something relatively insignificant.

Create shortcuts!

Operate on the customer's schedule.

What is your customer's schedule?

When in doubt — apologize.

Apologize even when the customer doesn't know you goofed.

Always make amends in excess of the slip-up.

Empower everyone to solve problems.

If you forget to include a biscuit, send a coupon for dinner.

If you can't seat them together in coach, bring them to first class.

If you can't deliver in time, throw in something extra, and don't be stingy.

When you say you are sorry, be so generous that there is no doubt that you mean it. You will create so much word-of-mouth that your mistake will be worth its weight in gold.

Having a system to handle mistakes is somewhat dangerous because it institutionalizes screw-ups. It may be saying, "We make so many mistakes that, rather than going to the root of the problem and seeking a solution, we'll just get better at fixing things."

You should have a system for resolving problems and responding to complaints. That system should focus on both resolving the immediate problem and preventing a future occurrence.

There is no better time for an out-of-proportion, unexpected response than when a customer is upset.

You can't hear if you don't listen. You can't listen from the office. Unheard problems are unresolved problems, and unresolved problems are lost sales. Period.

There is no greater way for a business to demonstrate status to customers than to know them by name.

Calling someone by name says, "You are special. I picked you out of the crowd. I remembered your name because you are important to me."

Make it a habit to learn the name of at least one new customer every day.

You can eat chicken anywhere, but you can have a good time only in a few places.

Showmanship is the art of giving products personality — yours!

If products can't qualify as a part of your own personality, you shouldn't sell them. Showmanship works only with products you believe in.

POS

How could you give your product personality?

Offering the customer an experience along with the product will be a significant competitive advantage.

Knowing that you are always going to be well treated adds value and the excitement of anticipation. Not knowing how that good treatment will be manifested adds a sense of mystery.

Not everyone wants to play. Some enjoy watching; others just want to get in and get out.

Showmanship directed to individuals should not begin until the customer has responded to a friendly probe.

To promote showmanship in any operation, you must:

- ☆ Hire "show-offs."
- ☆ Create opportunities for "show."
- ☆ Invite the customer to play.
- ☆ Reward showmanship.
- ☆ Be a "show-off!"

Regardless of who you hire or how you structure the job, it is unlikely that you will ever see employees inviting customers to play unless the boss leads the way.

Seven occasions when POS could be delivered:

1. Customers can be selected for random special treatment.
2. Potential customers can be chosen for random special treatment.
3. Events can be created specifically for customers.
4. Customer complaints can serve as cues for Positively Outrageous Service.
5. While customers are waiting, serve them outrageously.
6. After the sale is the perfect time to serve outrageously.
7. Watch for serendipitous cues as triggers for outrageous service.

If you intend to serve outrageously, do it publicly. Pick a time and place when you will be noticed.

Remember, POS results in compelling, positive word-of-mouth. What hasn't been said is that this word-of-mouth marketing can just as well come from someone who only observed as it can from someone who is directly involved.

Ready for POS marketing? Ask these questions first!:

☆ How do customers "arrive" at your business: walk-in, telephone, mail?
☆ What could you do that would be a surprise?
☆ Which vendors have the most invested in your success?
☆ What related businesses are good candidates for co-marketing?
☆ What local events, charities or groups are candidates for an outrageous promotion?

There are four components of a properly designed customer feedback system. It must:

- ☆ Provide immediate feedback to the customers.
- ☆ Require response from the top.
- ☆ Be sensitive to small issues.
- ☆ Always extend an offer.
- ☆ Lead to change.

Customer feedback systems must offer immediate response to both the customers and the organization.

A serious complaint deserves more than a follow-up letter. It deserves a personal phone call.

Sample your product. Occasionally ask your customers to try/test your product.

Your customers will be delighted to help, and they will revel in the opportunity to be heard and have an impact on your business.

Create world-class product sampling procedures.

Include customer comment cards with every order.

Post a direct phone number where customers can reach a manager or owner.

Call the customer. On a random basis, call and find out how you are doing. Know exactly what the customer has purchased and when. This act alone qualifies as Positively Outrageous Service.

A customer with a complaint has one basic thought: "Get this situation resolved and then I'll decide if you have another chance at my business."

Negative word-of-mouth is the one power every customer can exercise. Smart operators look for opportunities to creative positive word-of-mouth.

Every product comes with a promise. Complaints are nothing more than a breach of trust, real or imagined.

Customer response systems do more than make it easier to complain. They also make it easy for your customers to make suggestions and to praise good service.

You would be surprised at how many positive comments you can generate if you will just make responding easy.

POS

What can you do to make it easy for your customers to talk to you? *(Make a list.)*

Think of three ways to obtain and use testimonials!

Facts about lines:
- ☆ Lines are self-limiting.
- ☆ Lines can form only when customers arrive faster than they are served.
- ☆ Lines, once formed, persist indefinitely.
- ☆ Once service is delayed for any reason, every subsequent customer will wait for the length of the original delay.
- ☆ Lines are only as long as they appear.

Remember: Lines are self-limiting.

There is a point at which people will no longer join a line. That point is determined solely by the perceived value of what is at the end of the line.

Note: Lines can form only when customers arrive faster than they are served.

If a customer comes in and is served before another customer comes in, you cannot have a line. A line is only possible if a second customer arrives while the first customer is waiting for service or to complete the transaction.

Every time you see a line, you can be absolutely certain that at one time customers were arriving faster than they were being served.

If you have enough employees available to keep the line from growing, then you have enough available to have kept a line from forming in the first place.

What lines could you totally eliminate?

A fact: Lines, once formed, persist indefinitely.

As long as management exactly balances the ability of the system to serve against the speed of arrival of new customers, the line will persist forever. It cannot shrink because whenever a customer is served, a new customer takes her place.

To repeat: Once service is delayed for any reason, every subsequent customer will wait for the length of the original delay. Lines are only as long as they appear.

People do not study lines. They take a quick look and make an instant decision.

Snaked lines are shorter than straight lines.

A customer would rather be number three in a slow-moving line, than number nine in a fast line.

Service after the sale adds unexpected value to the product.

We rarely buy on price. Instead we buy an opportunity to feel good.

How could you make your customers feel even better?

The trend toward a service economy means that every day we are becoming a nation of first impressions. Our daily lives are a series of pop quizzes, instant decisions about whether or not we like a product or service.

The successful business will neither recruit nor hire employees who do not make a dynamite first impression as they go about the business of making customers feel good.

Find one knock-down, drag-out winning employee and you're hot on the trail of a whole flock of them! Start with your own winners. Ask them to help you recruit a friend. Don't worry. Winners like to work with other winners, and that's exactly who a winner will recommend.

P.S. We have never had an employee quit without notice or attempt to steal cash or merchandise who ran with a crowd of neat, polite friends. It just doesn't happen.

The best way to recruit winners is to let them come to you. They will if you establish a reputation for quality product and service, and for having a great place to work.

The losers in life don't expect much of either themselves or others. They will take a job almost anywhere. Why not? They don't expect to stay long anyway.

POS

Who do you expect to leave next? Why not help them?

When you promote in the community, you earn, as an important side benefit, top-of-mind positioning as a great place to work.

Winners have enough self-confidence and self-esteem to be picky about where they work. You want to position your business as a place for winners.

POS

Why would a winner want to work for you?

A full schedule means only that you have covered your shifts. It does not mean you are finished hiring. Your tactic should be to hire to the bench. Assemble a team and then continue to hire until you have a team of all-stars.

The problem with winners is that, like cops, they never seem to be around when you need one. If you are serious about hiring winners, you must be prepared to hire one anytime you find one.

You can't define a winner until you first define the job.

A winner is not a winner in every situation.

Your best employee may not always be your most successful.

How do you get ordinary employees to give meaningful Positively Outrageous Service?

- ☆ Hire outrageously.
- ☆ Model, measure and reward Positively Outrageous Service.
- ☆ Accord the employee personal status through title, freedom of choice, uniform or even ownership.
- ☆ Support outrageous mistakes, and reward outrageous service.

If an employee can do the job, but for some reason will not do it, all the training and experience in the world is of no value.

Every employee is motivated. They just may not be motivated to do what you want them to do.

POS

What turns on your employees?

If you have a great team, be careful not to contaminate it through careless hiring.

Make enough poor hiring decisions and not only will you lose customers, your winners will begin to feel out of place and move on to a place where they do fit again.

If you are unhappy with your present crew, you can raise the level of the water by hiring not to fit the personality of the team, but rather to fit the profile of the ideal.

POS

Define a winning employee in terms of your customers.

If you expect your employees to serve outrageously, you must be personally committed to serving as a visible standard.

You are the model against which employees compare their behavior.

Criticism stops behavior. Praise encourages behavior.

The tough job of enlightened management is to praise poor performers. Poor performance itself should not be the object of praise, but improved performance must be praised. It is the praise that makes continued improvement possible.

Create a "praise" feedback system. This could be a chart, E-mail notice, even a piece of candy!

Never lower your standards, but expect more every day.

Whatever you measure and reward, you will get.

The behavior you reward is always the behavior you get. People are not stupid. They do things that are rewarded.

How are you rewarding "stupid"?

Rewarding team effort has the effect of creating synergism.

Support outrageous mistakes. Reward Positively Outrageous Service.

The first mistake should always be free. It must be accompanied by encouragement to try again.

Management has only three simple responsibilities:
1. To clearly define the task at hand.
2. To remove obstacles and provide tools.
3. To say thank you for a job well done.

Management supplies the **GO-POWER**.

Goals	Short and in-your-face
Objectives	Daily lists
People	Put them in jobs where they can shine.
Ownership	Not just of the business but of the work!
Work design	Let people think.
Example	You are the visible standard — always.
Reward	Model, measure, reward great service.

Turned-on organizations start with turned-on leadership that defines the goals, sets the course and then goes on a crusade to recruit a battalion of like-minded followers.

For every hero of Positively Outrageous Service, there is an unsung hero of empowering leadership.

Turn chronic, unproductive, spirit-killing complaining into positive action with this simple line: "That's interesting. What are you willing to do to help solve the problem?"

Too few employees ever see the fruit of their labor. Too few employees are given whole tasks, tasks that have a beginning, middle and visible, measurable resolution.

POS

How are you modeling and measuring great performance?

Every job should have something that employees can count or otherwise measure as a symbol of tasks completed.

Feedback delayed is feedback denied.

POS

When and how do your employees learn how they are doing?

Excellent customer service occurs only when employees have an excellent, visible standard that they can imitate and against which they can compare their own behavior.

The good news is that the standard is always visible.

The bad news is that the visible standard is not always a visible standard of excellence.

What is your visible standard?

Recognition, reward, is a powerful tool. If you are not good at it, get good at it.

Your employees are watching. And so are your competitors!

Top causes of poor employee morale

1. Undesirable work environment
2. Improper materials or equipment
3. Lack of feedback
4. Inadequate benefits
5. Insufficient pay
6. No orientation, sales or product training
7. No organized approach or vision to direct efforts

Every day is evaluation day.

Making an example of excellent service gives permission to the uncommitted majority. It also gives them an avenue for the recognition and praise that we know people crave.

Employees do not leave work they love.

People love to work where people are loved.

Employee retention will improve the instant management compensation is linked to employee retention.

Public, on-the-spot praise becomes an important part of the training of both the praised and the public. I behave: You give instant feedback. I have no doubt about what must be done to get more praise!

Just as important, the co-worker standing nearby also has a learning experience. "I saw what you did. I saw how the boss reacted. I understand now exactly what I need to do to get some of that for myself."

Positively Outrageous Service will never permeate the entire organization until you create and implement a plan for turning over the organization to those who serve.

Positively Outrageous Service Predictor
Can you provide outrageous service?

1. I am proud of my accomplishments at work.
2. I have a great deal of confidence in my abilities.
4. I enjoy projects that call for rapid action.
5. I typically do well in pressure situations.
6. I enjoy jobs that permit movement and freedom.
7. I enjoy being surprised.
8. I enjoy entertaining guests.
9. I find it easy to make new friends.

10. I have a desire to be someone who is successful.
11. I would enjoy being famous.
12. People think of me as an energetic person.
13. Assuming the responsibilities of a leader feels good to me.
14. Many of my friends have a nonconventional lifestyle.

If you responded "true" to ten or more of these statements, you are confident, creative and chances are that you like people — all ingredients of outrageous talent.

Tips to getting POS:

- ☆ Be playful.
- ☆ Tip in advance.
- ☆ Award status.
- ☆ Assume.
- ☆ Use humor.
- ☆ Know when to settle for less than perfect.
- ☆ Help yourself.
- ☆ Never blame: just get it right.

About the Author

T. Scott Gross is America's expert on Positively Outrageously Service. A master of industrial-strength showmanship, Gross works with a who's who list of the world's most service-aggressive organizations.

He can write, but can he speak?

"We had a rating scale of 1–10 with 10 being fantastic, well worth it. You received 10s or higher. Positively great job." — *Bill Stock, Director of Training, Richfield Hotel Management*

To enjoy Scott in person, call
Tony Colao, Director, MasterMedia Speakers' Bureau
at (800) 453-2887.

Now if you still have questions about POS, the answers are as close as your computer...just jump on the information superhighway. Contact T. Scott Gross on CompuServe. His address is 72254,2160, or you can find him in the directory or fax him at (210) 634-2338 and expect a response within 48 hours!

For video or tape products, call (800) 635-7524 (M–F, 9 to 4 Central time) and ask for "Mom"!

MasterMedia Limited
17 East 89th Street
New York, NY 10128
(212) 260-5600
(800) 334-8232 please use Mastercard or Visa on 1-800 orders
(212) 546-7638 (fax)

OTHER BOOKS BY T. SCOTT GROSS

LEADING YOUR POSITIVELY OUTRAGEOUS SERVICE TEAM, by T. Scott Gross, provides a step-by-step formula for developing self-managing, excited service teams that put the customer first. T. Scott Gross tackles the question businesses everywhere are asking: "How do I get ordinary people to give world-class service?" A must-have for creating tomorrow's corporation today! ($12.95 paper)

POSITIVELY OUTRAGEOUS SERVICE AND SHOWMANSHIP: Industrial Strength Fun Makes Sales Sizzle!!!!, by T. Scott Gross, reveals the secrets of adding personality to any product or service. ($12.95 paper)

HOW TO GET WHAT YOU WANT FROM ALMOST ANYBODY, by T. Scott Gross, shows how to get great service, negotiate better prices, and always get what you pay for. ($9.95 paper)

OTHER MASTERMEDIA BUSINESS BOOKS

A SEAT AT THE TABLE: An Insider's Guide for America's New Women Leaders, by Patricia Harrison, provides practical and insightful advice for women who are interested in serving on a board of directors, playing a key role in politics and becoming a policy- or opinion-maker in public or private sectors. This is one book every woman needs to own. ($19.95 hardbound)

LIFETIME EMPLOYABILITY: How to Become Indispensable, by Carole Hyatt, is both a guide through the mysteries of the business universe brought down to earth and a handbook to help you evaluate your attitudes, your skills and your goals. Through expert advice and interviews of nearly 200 men and women whose lives have changed because their jobs or goals shifted, Lifetime Employability is designed to increase your staying power in today's down-sized economy. ($12.95 paper)

OUT THE ORGANIZATION: New Career Opportunities for the 1990's, by Robert and Madeleine Swain, is written for the millions of Americans whose jobs are no longer safe, whose companies are not loyal, and who face futures of uncertainty. It gives advice on finding a new job or starting your own business. ($12.95 paper)

BEYOND SUCCESS: How Volunteer Service Can Help You Begin Making a Life Instead of Just a Living, by John F. Raynolds III and Eleanor Raynolds, C.B.E., is a unique how-to book targeted at business and professional people considering volunteer work, senior citizens who wish to fill leisure time meaningfully, and students trying out various career options. The book is filled with interviews with celebrities, CEOs, and average citizens who talk about the benefits of service work. ($19.95 cloth)

WORK WITH ME! How to Make the Most of Office Support Staff, by Betsy Lazary, shows you how to find, train, and nurture the "perfect" assistant and how to best utilize your support staff professionals. ($9.95 paper)

THE LOYALTY FACTOR: Building Trust in Today's Workplace, by Carol Kinsey Goman, Ph.D., offers techniques for restoring commitment and loyalty in the workplace. ($9.95 paper)

BREATHING SPACE: Living and Working at a Comfortable Pace in a Sped-Up Society, by Jeff Davidson, helps readers to handle information and activity overload, and gain greater control over their lives. ($10.95 paper)

TWENTYSOMETHING: Managing and Motivating Today's New Work Force, by Lawrence J. Bradford, Ph.D., and Claire Raines, M.A., examines the work orientation of the younger generation, offering managers in businesses of all kinds a practical guide to better understand and supervise their young employees. ($22.95 cloth)

BALANCING ACTS! Juggling Love, Work, Family, and Recreation, by Susan Schiffer Stautberg and Marcia L. Worthing, provides strategies to achieve a balanced life by reordering priorities and setting realistic goals. ($12.95 paper)

STEP FORWARD: Sexual Harassment in the Workplace, What You Need to Know, by Susan L. Webb, presents the facts for identifying the tell-tale signs of sexual harassment on the job, and how to deal with it. ($9.95 paper)

TEAMBUILT: Making Teamwork Work, by Mark Sanborn, teaches business how to improve productivity, without increasing resources or expenses, by building teamwork among employers. ($19.95 cloth)

POS

Don't forget to love one another!